50 STATES TO CELEBRATE

Celebrating
ARIZONA

www.hmhbooks.com

The text of this book is set in Weidemann.
The display type is set in Bernard Gothic.
The illustrations are drawn with pencil and colored digitally.
The maps are pen, ink, and watercolor.

Photograph of ringtails on page 32 © 2013 by Photodisc/Getty Images
Photograph of cactus wren on page 32 © 2013 by Natphotos/Digital Vision/Getty Images
Photograph of Saguaro cactus blossoms on page 32 © 2013 by Raquel Baranow as "Saguaro
    Cactus blossoms" under Creative Commons license 2.0

Library of Congress Cataloging-in-Publication Data
Bauer, Marion Dane.
Celebrating Arizona / by Marion Dane Bauer ; illustrated by C.B. Canga.
p. cm. — (50 states to celebrate) (Green light readers level 3)
ISBN 978-0-544-04387-9 paper over board
ISBN 978-0-544-04419-7 trade paper
1. Arizona—Juvenile literature. I. Canga, C. B., illustrator. II. Title.
F811.3.B38 2013
979.1—dc23
2012039312

Manufactured in China
SCP 10 9 8 7 6 5 4 3 2 1
4500424124

50 STATES TO CELEBRATE

Celebrating
ARIZONA

Written by **Marion Dane Bauer**
Illustrated by **C. B. Canga**

sandpiper

Houghton Mifflin Harcourt
Boston   New York

ARIZONA

LAKE MEAD

GRAND CANYON NATIONAL PARK

MONUMENT VALLEY ~ Navajo Nation

HOOVER DAM

COLORADO RIVER

CANYON DE CHELLY

SLIDE ROCK STATE PARK

Flagstaff

PAINTED DESERT

SEDONA CANYON

Scottsdale

★ Phoenix

SONORAN DESERT

Tucson

N
W   E
S

What a colorful sunrise!
What an awesome scene!
Hi, I'm Mr. Geo,
and here I am in Arizona,
the Grand Canyon State.

Washington

Montana

North Dakota

Oregon

Idaho

South Dakota

Wyoming

Nebraska

Nevada

Utah

Colorado

Kansas

California

Arizona

New Mexico

Okla

Texas

PACIFIC OCEAN

CANADA

MEXICO

Alaska

*NOT TO SCALE

Hawaii

*NOT TO SCALE

Let's find Arizona on the map.
Look west of New Mexico and south
of Utah.

Now look east of California and Nevada.

Look north of Mexico.

That's Arizona!

3

Here I am at the Grand Canyon,
looking down
. . . and down
. . . and down.
See that stream down there?
That's the mighty Colorado River.

This mule is going to take me
all the way to the bottom.
It's going to be a very bumpy ride.
I hope he doesn't trip!

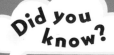

Did you know?

It took about six million years for water
to carve this enormous **canyon**.

At last, I'm at the bottom of the canyon!
It's time for a gentle float down the Colorado River.
Whoops! No one told me about these wild **rapids**.

In 1869, John Wesley Powell became the first explorer to successfully lead an expedition down the Colorado River through the Grand Canyon.

The **Anasazi** were among the first people in Arizona.

At Canyon de Chelly, we can see how they lived. Just imagine! This wall carving is more than 1,000 years old!

The Anasazi also carved amazing cliff-side cities into the rock.

The modern Pueblo tribes, including Hopi, Zuni, Acoma, and Laguna, descended from the Anasazi.

I've always wanted to tour Monument Valley in the Navajo Nation.

Lots of movies have been filmed here.

That must be why it looks so familiar!

The Navajo form the largest Native American nation in the United States.

Rocks take such interesting shapes here.
Can you guess why that rock is called the
Left Mitten?

Up, up, and away!
How about a hot air balloon ride over
Sedona Canyon?
I can see why this place is called
Red Rock Country!

Next stop! A natural waterslide at Slide Rock
State Park.
It's not too far from an apple orchard!
Splash! Swish! Yum!

Long ago, people learned to **irrigate** this land
to farm it. Today, irrigation helps Arizona
grow fruits and vegetables all year long.

Newcomers often move to Arizona for the sunny climate.
But Native Americans have been here much, much longer.
Both desert Apache and Navajo used to live in cool earth **hogans**.
Some still do.

Navajo artists are known for their woven blankets and rugs and for their silver and **turquoise** jewelry.

The Hopi lived in **pueblo** villages.
My Hopi friend invited me to visit
his modern pueblo-style home.
It is built of stone and **adobe**.

The first Spanish explorers arrived in the 1540s.
They had heard amazing stories about
Seven Cities of Gold.
More explorers came, hoping to get rich.
But no one found gold at this time.

Prospectors discovered gold in Arizona in the mid-1800s. They also found silver and copper.

Spanish priests came later and built **missions**.
The festival at the Mission San Jose de Tumacacori
celebrates Arizona's European, Spanish, Mexican,
and Native American **cultures**.
What do you think is in this **piñata**?

The town of Tombstone developed around a silver mine in 1877.

It was a big part of the **Wild West** era.

Miners, pioneers, cowboys, and outlaws!

All came seeking adventure.

I did too! Climb aboard!

Mining is still a big industry in Arizona.
The state produces more **copper** than all other
states combined.
Today, I'm visiting the old Copper Queen Mine.
This tour is taking me 1,500 feet below ground.

The dome of the state capitol building
in Phoenix is covered with copper.

About half of Arizona is desert.
The Painted Desert, in the northeast,
is striped in reds, browns, purples, and blues.
The Sonoran Desert, in the southwest,
is one of the biggest deserts in North America.
It stretches into California and Mexico.

The colors in the Painted Desert come from different minerals in the soil.

Even hot, dry deserts are filled with plants and animals.

Joshua trees and creosote bushes

live in some deserts.

Wild burros, **javelinas,** and rattlesnakes do too.

And watch out for gila monsters and rolling

tumbleweeds!

Many different kinds of cactus plants grow
in Arizona.
The saguaro reaches its "arms" up to the sky.

The Saguaro cactus grows very slowly,
less than an inch a year.

Guess what musical instrument the
organ pipe cactus looks like!
People and animals can eat the fruit of the
prickly pear cactus.
I'm not sure I know how!

What is more precious in a desert than silver or gold?

If you said water, you're right!

Arizona has many rivers, but some run low or dry much of the year.

Did you know?

The Hoover Dam is located between Arizona and Nevada. It created a huge reservoir called Lake Mead.

Dams create lakes and **reservoirs**.
The collected water **irrigates** crops and brings the
desert to life.
Water is fun to play in, too!

Arizona is filled with natural wonders. But the cities also have much to offer. Today I'm learning all about Native American tribes of the Southwest at the Heard Museum in Phoenix.

The Heard Museum is home to hundreds of historic Hopi kachina dolls.

In Tucson the Arizona-Sonora Desert Museum
teaches respect for the desert world.
I met a bobcat and an ocelot there.
And a tarantula, too!

When I'm in Arizona I love rooting for the home team.
For baseball, it's the Diamondbacks.

The Diamondbacks won the World Series in 2001 when the team was only four years old.

The Phoenix Suns shoot hoops.
The Phoenix Coyotes play hockey.
And the Arizona Cardinals love to score
touchdowns.
Go, team, go!

We began our visit to Arizona with a sunrise.
Let's end it with the night sky.
Few places in the world show off the stars
better than the dry, clear air of Arizona.

I even saw Mars close up through a
huge telescope at the observatory.
Wow! What a sky!
Wow! What a state!

Fast Facts About Arizona

Nickname: The Grand Canyon State.

State motto: *Ditat Deus* (God enriches).

State capital: Phoenix.

Other major cities: Tucson, Flagstaff, Scottsdale.

Year of statehood: 1912.

State mammal: Ringtail.   **State bird:** Cactus wren.

State flower: Saguaro cactus blossom.   **State flag:**

Population: Nearly 6.4 million people, according to the 2010 U.S. census.

Fun fact: In 1903 President Theodore Roosevelt said of the Grand Canyon, "Leave it as it is. You cannot improve on it. The ages have been at work on it, and man can only mar it."

Dates in Arizona History

1150–1300: Anasazi carve and live in communities of cliff dwellings.

1540: Spanish explorers arrive in Arizona.

1629: Spanish priests establish a mission among the Hopi.

1680: The Pueblo and Hopi people rebel against Spanish rule.

1775: Tucson is founded.

1821: Mexico wins independence from Spain.

1848: Mexican-American War ends. The United States takes control of northern Arizona.

1853: The United States purchases southern Arizona.

1859: The first Native American reservation is established in Arizona.

1863: Arizona territory is created.

1869: John Wesley Powell leads an expedition down the Colorado River through the Grand Canyon.

1935: The Hoover Dam opens on the border of Arizona and Nevada.

1912: Arizona becomes the 48th state.

1919: The Grand Canyon becomes a national park.

1948: Native Americans in Arizona get the right to vote.

1981: Sandra Day O'Connor, an Arizonan, becomes the first woman to be named to the Supreme Court.

2001: The Arizona Diamondbacks win the World Series.

Activities

1. **LOCATE** the two states on Arizona's western border on the map on pages 2 and 3. Then, **SAY** each state's name out loud.

2. **DRAW** a picture of a wall carving that depicts something about Arizona. On the back, explain why you created the design.

3. **SHARE** two facts you learned about Arizona with a family member or friend.

4. **PRETEND** you are junior tour guide at the Grand Canyon. The kids in your tour group have lots of questions about the state of Arizona. Answer the following questions for them correctly and you will be honored as "Most Valuable Tour Guide of the Month."

    a. **WHO** was the first person to lead an expedition down the Colorado River through the Grand Canyon?

    b. **WHAT** kind of homes did the Apache and Navajo live in?

    c. **WHEN** did the first Spanish explorers arrive in Arizona?

    d. **WHERE** is the Hoover Dam located?

    e. **WHICH** kind of cactus has "arms" that reach up toward the sky?

5. **UNJUMBLE** these words that have something to do with Arizona. Write your answers on a separate sheet of paper.

    a. **NYCAON** (HINT: It's made of rock)

    b. **LBOPEU** (HINT: A type of Native American home)

    c. **PEPOCR** (HINT: a metal mined in Arizona)

    d. **KRTTSAEENLA** (HINT: a desert creature)

    e. **MTTSOOENB** (HINT: an old mining town)

Glossary

adobe: a brick made of dried clay and straw. (p. 15)

Anasazi: an ancient Native American people who lived in area of the Southwest where the states of Arizona, New Mexico, Colorado, and Utah now meet; these people are also called Ancestral Puebloans. (p. 8)

canyon: a deep valley with steep, rocky walls on both sides. Canyons are formed when rivers or streams wash away soil and rock over a long period of time. The Grand Canyon in Arizona is 277 miles long and 18 miles wide. (p. 5)

copper: a reddish-brown metal that is easy to mold. (p. 19)

culture: the customs, beliefs, and ways of living shared by a group of people. (p. 17)

dam: a barrier built across a waterway to control the flow of water or to create a lake for storing water. (p. 25)

hogan: a one-room dwelling made of logs and covered with earth. (p. 14)

irrigate: to supply land or crops with water using streams, ditches, pipes, or sprinklers. (pp. 13 and 25)

javelina: a dark gray animal that looks like a hairy pig; the javelina, also called a collared peccary, can be found in the deserts of the Southwest. (p. 21)

Left Mitten (Butte): a rock formation in Arizona's Monument Valley that resembles a mitten that would be worn on a person's left hand. A butte is a steep hill that rises sharply and has a small flat top; the word *butte* rhymes with *cute.* (p. 11)

mission: a place where religious and cultural ideas can be taught. (p. 17)

piñata: a decorated container that is usually filled with candy and toys and hung from a rope at parties; people wearing blindfolds take turns trying to break open piñatas with a stick. The word *piñata* comes from Spanish. (p. 17)

prospector: a person who searches an area for gold, silver, copper, oil, or some other valuable mineral deposit. (p. 16)

pueblo: a village made up of stone and adobe buildings, usually with flat roofs and often several stories high. (p. 15)

rapids: a place in a river where the water flows very fast. (p. 6)

reservoir: a pond or lake that is used for storing water. (p. 25)

turquoise: a greenish-blue stone that is often used in jewelry. (p. 14)

Wild West: a way of referring to the western United States during the frontier era, because of a lack of laws and rough behavior. (p. 18)

Answers to activities on page 34:

1) Nevada and California; 2) wall carving designs will vary; 3) answers will vary; 4a) John Wesley Powell; 4b) hogans; 4c) 1540s; 4d) between Arizona and Nevada; 4e) saguaro; 5a) CANYON; 5b) PUEBLO; 5c) COPPER; 5d) RATTLESNAKE; 5e) TOMBSTONE.